Mindfulness

A Thirty Days Plan for Breaking the Cycle of Anxiety, Stress and Unhappiness

COPYRIGHT NOTICE

Limits of Liability / Disclaimer

We tried our best to make sure that the information presented in this book is useful. However, you as a reader must know that the information provided here does not constitute legal or medical or professional advice of any kind.

The author of this book shall in no event be held liable for any kind or type of losses or damages whatsoever and that including, without limitation, consequential loss or damage, either directly or indirectly by using this book.

Table of Contents

INTRODUCTION...7

SECTION I UNDERSTANDING ANXIETY, STRESS, AND UNHAPPINESS...13

Chapter 1 What Exactly is Anxiety 14

    The Never-Ending Cycle of Anxiety 19

    Anxiety Disorders...20

    Symptoms of Anxiety...22

    Types of Anxiety Disorder.......................................26

Chapter 2 Understanding Stress 35

    Common Signs and Symptoms of Stress........................38

        What Really Causes Stress? 40

    Anxiety vs. Stress...42

    Depression/Unhappiness 45

    How to identify if you are depressed 46

    Symptoms of Depression..47

SECTION II BREAKING THE CYCLE OF ANXIETY, STRESS, AND UNHAPPINESS 49

Chapter 3 Energy Consumers and Energy Providers.........50

    Can I Still Enjoy Myself? 51

    Empty the Mind to Sleep..59

Chapter 4 Positive Thoughts...66

Rational Emotive Therapy 67

Practicing Positive Thinking 74

Chapter 5 Set Realizable Daily Targets..............................76

What are Your Goals? 86

SECTION III THE POWER OF MEDITATION 87

Chapter 6 Meditation and Deep Breathing for Anxiety Relief...88

Deep Breathing..89

The Power of Meditation..92

Chapter 7 How Meditation Breaks the Cycle of Anxiety ...95

Meditation Disrupts Anxious Thought Patterns 95

Meditation for the Relief of Anxiety 99

Practicing Mindfulness Meditation...............................100

Meditations to Help Banish Stress 102

Combating Anxiety Attacks with This Meditation.......106

Chapter 8 Adopting a Positive Mindset and Resilience...109

How to Build Your Resilience 110

Always be Thankful 112

Embrace Happiness 114

Chapter 9 Switching Off is Possible 118

How do you Handle Your Addiction?............................124

Chapter 10 Effectively Managing Your Time 125

    Saying No 129

  Technology Use, Depression, Fatigue, and Stress 130

  Chapter 11 Sleep as a Strategy for Dealing with Anxiety, Stress, and Depression 133

  How sleep deprivation Causes Anxiety 134

  Dealing with the Sleep Debt-Related Anxiety 137

Final Thoughts 140

  About the Author 142

INTRODUCTION

Can you recall the very last time you laid down and fought tooth and nail to forgo some thoughts? Indeed you needed and wanted to just have a peaceful night rest without unnecessary disturbing thoughts. You close your eyes to sleep but suddenly experience an immense number of thoughts trooping into your head with renewed vigor. Nothing, however, seemed to work. At this very point, you try consoling yourself by saying don't worry but again, you are worrying even more than before. You soon discover you're getting drained as a new dawn knocks. This anxious state of mind takes away your happiness and keeps you stressed out.

Waking up to the new day that should be full of life and activities, you find yourself struggling to keep your eyes open to carry-out the events of the day. You cannot concentrate on anything. Your brain is outdated due to the stress caused by anxiety which has conclusively led to your unhappiness.

There is something common among all human beings and that is the deep desire to live a happy life. Happiness is sweet when it can be sustained and protected. When our day is clouded with a constant struggle to be less anxious, stress and unhappiness can even worsen the situation altogether.

Everyone once in a while may have days like these when all you want is just to sleep without that feeling of anxiety, stress, and unhappiness. However, it is essential to note that recovery is possible and not far away.

According to Prof. Mark Williams and Danny Penman Ph.D. in their 30 years study of anxiety, stress, and depression, they discovered the secret to happiness and how you can successfully tackle anxiety, stress, and depression. In their research, they discovered the happiness and peace that get into your bones and promotes a deep-seated authentic love of life, seeping into everything you do and come to help you overcome everything and anything that the world throws at you.

In this book "A Thirty Days Plan for breaking the Cycle of Anxiety, Stress, and Unhappiness", we shall extensively discuss how one can overcome anxiety, stress, and unhappiness in just thirty days.

If you are reading this book, then you may have at certain times wondered to yourself why the peace and happiness you so much sought for seem to always slip from your grasp. Why the entire world seems to be running after or chasing after something resulting in anxiety, stress, and unhappiness due to their inability to achieve their targets.

We shall discuss the terms Anxiety, Stress and Unhappiness and pinpoint how it all affects our day to day interaction with others and how our own peace and joyfulness is so much distorted by our thoughts. Our disposition always either wax or wane. That's how a man was created. However, our thought pattern can deepen a short-term depression or emotion into a longer period of anxiety, stress, and unhappiness. A brief period of anger, sadness anxiousness can end up catapulting you into an 'unhappy mood' that reshapes your whole day.

Recent scientific discoveries have outlined how emotional switches can lead to long-term unhappiness, severe nervousness, and even depression. But more importantly, these scientific findings have also shown the path to becoming a happier person as it indicated that:

- Your reaction to feeling sad, anxious and unhappy is what does the damage and not the mood in itself.
- The attempt to free yourself from a bad mood or episode of unhappiness – of working out why you're sad and what can be done – often times makes things worse.

As soon as you comprehend the working of the mind, it becomes clearer why we suffer from bouts of unhappiness, stress, and anxiety.

When you become unhappy, it's proper to try and seek ways to get unhappiness behind you. You feel the need to ascertain what caused the unhappiness and search for the solution. In the process, you can possibly search out past regrets and summon up future doubts. This reality further reduces your mood. It mostly does take a long time before you start feeling bad for the failure to cheer yourself up. That 'self-critic' which is innate in us begins to whisper that it's your fault, that you should try harder whatever the cost. You suddenly begin to feel disconnected from your innate wise part of your being. Soon, you get lost in continual reproach and self-judgment; blaming yourself for not meeting standards and for not becoming who you wished to be.

Our mind is innately connected to our memory; hence we get drawn into these emotional tantrums. Your mind is continually traveling through the bout of memories to discover the ones that reverberate our current disturbing state. For instance, if you are endangered, your mind instantly travels through memories of when you were last endangered, so as to cite similarities and detect means of escape. This event happens instantly, almost without you noticing. This is an innate survival skill sharpened by million years of evolution. This instinct is almost impossible to stop.

Same is true with anxiety, stress, and unhappiness. It is not abnormal to feel a little sad once in a while, but most times a few unhappy thoughts can set off battalions of sad memories, negative emotions, and cruel conclusions. Not long, hours or days can be ravaged by unhelpful self-critique thoughts for instance; what is wrong with me? My life is a mess, what happens when they discover what failure I have become? So on and so forth goes the thoughts.

So in a clear and identifiable way, this book will provide you with realistic step by step insights into overcoming anxiety, stress, and unhappiness in thirty days and how you can enthusiastically renew your life.

SECTION I UNDERSTANDING ANXIETY, STRESS, AND UNHAPPINESS

Chapter 1 What Exactly is Anxiety

Every one of us will always feel anxious once in a while and that's a normal condition. In fact, it's believed that a certain level of anxiety is not only normal but also helpful in certain situations. Are you wondering how anxiety can be helpful after all the problems associated with it? It's understandable for people having anxiety disorder to be skeptical about anxiety being helpful in any way, however, your response to danger is often as a result of anxiety. Anxious feelings happen to be our normal response to a condition where we are under pressure like speaking in front of a large audience or sitting for an exam. It motivates us to take action in the face of danger.

So, what is anxiety? It's an emotion that is associated with a state of inner turmoil that is unpleasant and often characterized by nervous behavior like rumination, pacing back and forth and somatic complaints. It can also be described as a subjectively distasteful feeling of fear of certain events anticipated to take place like the feeling of imminent death. Unlike fear which is our response to the perceived or real threat, anxiety is the expectation of a future threat. It actually has to do with feelings of worry, and uneasiness. Anxiety is generally perceived as an overreaction to circumstances that are just subjectively viewed as menacing. Anxiety is usually accompanied by restlessness, muscular tension, and concentration problems. Although as I earlier mentioned, anxiety has several benefits, however, when it has become a regular experience, then you may really have anxiety disorder. To find out more about anxiety disorder, check chapter... Individuals experiencing anxiety may actually withdraw from the situations that initially caused the anxiety. So in summary, anxiety is:

A state of uncertainty, apprehension, and fear as a result of anticipation of a fantasized or realistic threatening situation or event which often ends up impairing psychological and physical functioning. It's a state of apprehension and uneasiness regarding future uncertainties.

So anxiety happens when we think or act in an apprehensive way. Now, anxiety is not by a genetic, chemical or biological problem but it's a product of a specific style of behavior.

Anxiety could be perceived by some individuals as a disease, but it's not a disease. It's just a psychological and emotional state that we find ourselves when we behave apprehensively. The main cause of anxiety is an apprehensive behavior like worry. Generally, we become scared when we think that something or someone we care about (ourselves included) could be in harm's way. Unlike people that are anxious normally, overly anxious persons perceive danger more frequently and to a greater extent than those that are not so anxious and this overly anxious behavior is responsible for the problems we experience with anxiety. Although the negative effects of chronic anxiety may feel like an uncontrollable, random and unknown health problem, there are several ways to deal with problematic anxiety effectively, however, a lot of people find it difficult to deal with the problem of anxiety. Never mind, you will discover effective

16

ways to deal with anxiety and stress which will also usher in happiness into your life.

Why does It last so Long?

Often times, people suffer from anxiety for a prolonged time and it gradually turns into a life problem leading to a never-ending circle. This is caused by several factors: Some people have an anxious personality making them worry all the time. Such people will probably have a habit of feeling anxious most of the time. There are also a set of people who passed through stressful situations for several years and finally developed the habit of constantly being anxious. Let's take a look at some reasons why anxiety tends to persist for long.

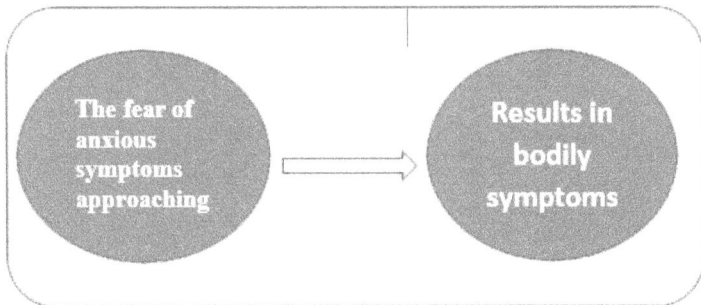

The Fear of "Fear"

When you have experienced anxiety before in a certain situation, there is a possibility that you will predict feeling anxious again. This will frighten you because of the symptoms you once experienced and this in turn actually causes you to experience the same symptoms you are afraid of.

The Never-Ending Cycle of Anxiety

Most times when we experience the bodily symptoms of anxiety, it tends to be unpleasant, unusual and frightening. In fact, people tend to react by thinking that something terrible is physically wrong with them or something nasty is going to happen to them. Guess what, this leads to more symptoms leading to a vicious circle which will never end until steps are taken to resolve it.

Thoughts
Now I'm in serios trouble

The feeling of bodily symptoms
Heart starts pounding
Breath incresaes

Feeling anxious

Thoughts
Something terrible is going
to happen to me now

Avoidance

The moment a vicious circle of anxiety has been established, people will harbor lots of anxious thoughts leading to an increase in the anxiety symptoms. In such situations, the easiest way to cope with anxiety which people wrongly adopt is avoidance. Naturally, we tend to avoid things that we perceive as dangerous however, the kind of things that people often avoid when they experience anxiety are usually not the real dangers, rather things like crowded places, talking to people, busy shops, etc. Things like these are not dangerous, rather, they are part of the things that make life easier and fun. Life can be difficult and stressful when these things are avoided and such avoidance often leads to a great loss of confidence and this will, in turn, affect the way you feel about yourself generally. Whenever you dislike the way you feel regarding yourself, your anxiousness increases - and the circle continues!

Anxiety Disorders

They are a group of different mental disorders that are characterized by great feelings of fear and anxiety Did you know that anxiety disorders happen to be the most common mental illness in the world including the United States the United Kingdom and many other developed and developing countries? It is believed that it actually affects adults who are 18 years or more (about 40 million or 18.1 percent of the population in the US alone). Well, the good news is that anxiety disorders are much treatable though only 36.9 percent of people suffering from it get treatment. Available data clearly provides evidence to prove that individuals experiencing anxiety disorders are 3-5 times more prone to check a doctor and six times more likely to receive treatment for psychiatric disorders than other individuals that are not suffering from the health issue. So what causes anxiety disorders? Well, it's a combination of both environmental and genetic factors. Among the risk factors include a family history of mental disorders, a history of child abuse and poverty. Also, anxiety disorders usually occur with different mental disorders especially substance use disorder, major depressive disorder and personality disorder. In order for anxiety disorder to be diagnosed, it should meet certain criteria:

- Its symptoms basically need to have been noticed for a minimum of six months
- There should be decreased functioning and it should be more than what would be expected for the situation.

Symptoms of Anxiety

The symptoms of anxiety disorder and anxiety are the same, however, there exists just one difference which is: while anxiety and its persistence grows, so will the intensity, number, duration frequency, and type of anxiety increase. Knowing some of the symptoms of anxiety will help you easily determine whether you're in any way suffering from anxiety disorder. Anxiety disorder has been treated earlier in this chapter. So, let's take a look at some common symptoms of anxiety.

Symptoms

Feelings	- The feeling of fear (especially in anticipation of facing certain events, situations or objects) - The panic that's overwhelming and uncontrollable - Being worried about the physical symptoms (e.g. the fear of an undiagnosed medical issue) - Overwhelmed - Constantly on the edge, nervous and tense - Dread- scared that something bad may likely happen
Physical	- Shortness of breath - Pains and muscle tension - Racing heart

- Vomiting or pain in the stomach
- Experiencing trouble with sleep- having difficulty sleeping, staying asleep or having a restless sleep
- Dizzy and lightheaded
- Sweating and shaking
- Finding it difficult to concentrate
- Having the feeling of being separated from your surroundings
- Hot or cold flushes
- Numbness or tingling

Behavior
- Being easily startled

- Having the urge to do certain rituals in order to relieve anxiety
- Finding it difficult to make decisions
- Withdrawing from or avoiding fear objects/situations that might have caused anxiety
- Not being assertive (avoiding eye contact)

Thoughts

You may have any of the following thoughts:

- I'm about to die
- Unwanted or intrusive thoughts
- I'm unable to control myself
- I'm always judged by people
- Finding it difficult to desist from worrying
- I'm about dying

25

- Experiencing upsetting flashbacks or dreams of the traumatic event

Types of Anxiety Disorder

Let's take a look at the most common types of anxiety disorder

Generalized Anxiety Disorder (GAD)

We are always anxious from time to time and we often have several things to worry about. But for individuals that experience generalized anxiety disorder, they frequently and intensely worry about a lot of things. Such people are often regarded as worrywarts several years ago. When you suffer from generalized anxiety disorder, it doesn't mean that your level of anxiety is worse, it only implies that you worry about many things and more often. If you're suffering from generalized anxiety, then you are likely to experience the following:

- Finding it difficult to make decisions or remembering commitments because you're unable to fully concentrate and you're fully preoccupied with worry
- When you're worried about the daily issues of life for a period of six months or even more
- Having an appearance that is strained with an increase in sweating from the feet, hand and axillae Could also be tearful which suggests depression
- Constantly being worried about your feeling almost everyday
- Experiencing several psychological, physical and emotional symptoms of anxiety

In the US for instance, generalized anxiety disorder affects about 6.8 million adults which is 3.1 percent of the population. Women are usually twice more likely to suffer from GAD than men.

Panic Attack Disorder (PAD)

Also known as panic disorder, it is characterized by a person having brief attacks of serious terror and apprehension which usually results in confusion, nausea, shaking, dizziness and/or difficulty in breathing. The APA defines panic attacks as discomfort or fear that suddenly arises and peaks in less than a period of 10 minutes and can last for hours.

Often times, stress, irrational thoughts, fear, strenuous exercise and having the fear of the unknown triggers panic attacks. Sometimes, what triggers panic attacks is unclear and it can be triggered without warning. Avoiding the trigger is one good way to avoid the attack. Apart from the recurrent unexpected panic attacks, in order to diagnose panic disorder, the attacks need to have chronic consequences such as persistent fear of subsequent attacks, worry over the implication of potential attack and major changes in behavior that's related to attacks. Individuals who experience PAD encounter symptoms that are often not connected to specific panic episodes. People suffering from panic disorder may experience changes in their heartbeat which often leads

28

them to think that something might be wrong with their heart. In the course of experiencing panic attacks, there is also hyper-vigilance (having an increased consciousness of the functioning of the body) and a perceived physiological change. This could even be perceived as a likely life-threatening illness. Common symptoms associated with PAD include:

- Racing heart
- Super sensitive senses and nerves
- Muscle weakness
- An intense feeling of doom and gloom
- Lightheadedness
- Weak in the knees
- Pins and needles
- Increased stimulation
- Throat tightness
- Having a feeling that you're about to lose control
- Feeling overwhelmed
- Heightened fear and apprehension
- Nervous stomach

- Trembling
- Sudden and strong urge to escape
- Having a feeling that makes you think you're going crazy
- Heart palpitations
- Profusely sweating

Separation Anxiety Disorder (SepAD)

It has to do with having excessive anxiety feelings that are wrong especially after separation from a place or person. Although being anxious because of separation is a normal aspect of child development, however, when it's in excess or inappropriate, it can be regarded as a disorder. It affects an estimate of 7 percent of adults and 4 percent of children, however, the childhood cases often tend to be more severe. Early treatment of a child is the best way to prevent the problem. When it comes to separation anxiety disorder, parents often reinforce the anxiety since they lack the skills to properly help the child overcome it.

Obsessive-Compulsive Disorder (OCD)

It is described as experiencing unwanted thoughts and actions that appear quite difficult and impossible to stop. Although many people worry, people that suffer from obsessive-compulsive disorder have this feeling that they can't just stop worrying and if they eventually do, then something nasty will happen.

People experiencing this kind of disorder actually knows fully well that the symptoms does not seem real, but they still battle with the thoughts and also the behavior. Sometimes, the symptoms they experience may have to do with certain external events they are afraid of (like a thief grabbing their money because the door wasn't locked) or they may bother themselves of not behaving properly.

Some of the risk factors of OCD include higher socioeconomic class, family history, not being in paid employment or being single- though that could also be as a result of the disorder. Obsessive-compulsive disorder is chronic and about 20 percent of people suffering from OCD will overcome and over time, the symptoms may reduce for most people (about 50 percent). Some of the symptoms of OCD include:

- Underlying fear
- Nervousness
- Sleep issues
- Relentless worry
- An underlying sense of danger
- Agitation
- The inability to self-soothe

Social Anxiety Disorder (SAD)

This anxiety disorder relates to an intense fear and avoidance of humiliation, social interaction, negative public scrutiny, or public embarrassment. It can be specific to a particular social situation like public speaking or experienced in almost all social interactions. Some of the symptoms of social anxiety disorder include: including blushing, physical symptoms, difficulty speaking, sweating and blushing. People suffering from social anxiety usually try to avoid the source of their anxiety and it can result in complete social isolation.

Post-Traumatic Stress Disorder

This is a type of anxiety stress disorder that is caused by a traumatic experience. PTSD is usually as a result of an extreme circumstance like child abuse, hostage situations, serious accident, natural disaster, combat, rape, bullying, etc. Also, it can be as a result of chronic exposure to severe stressors. The memories, nightmares, flashbacks, and night terrors of the traumatic event can be so clear that they trigger anxious reactions and symptoms that are seemingly uncontrollable.

Most times, people suffering from post-traumatic stress disorder feel helpless in wiping out such negative nightmares, memories, flashbacks and night terrors. Some individuals suffering from PTSD often say that it's like having a panic attack 24/7 and having a feeling that nothing can be done to change it. Well, it can be changed, just read on to find out simple and effective ways to deal with it. Some of the symptoms of PTSD include:

- Avoiding others

- Constant anxiety and worry
- Having a persistent internal struggle
- Recurring flashbacks, memories, and nightmares that appear unstoppable
- Having a persistent feeling of insecurity and at risk
- Always avoiding situations that are linked with reminders and the traumatic event itself
- Underlying fear and trepidation
- Avoiding certain situations that may remind you of the event
- Being overly vigilant especially in uncertain situations

Chapter 2 Understanding Stress

While trying to deal with stress, it's important to first understand what it's all about. Sometimes, stress, anxiety, and depression can be mixed up, however, they are separate health issues that people experience and if you're serious about dealing with these issues, then you need to first understand them and their symptoms. As earlier mentioned, stress isn't really a bad thing as always portrayed, mankind wouldn't have survived without our ability to feel stress.

Stress was an indicator for our cavemen ancestors because it alerted them of a potential danger like an encroaching lion or a poisonous snake. Basically, it is a physical response to life issues. We tend to switch instantly to a fight or flight mode when our body is stressed since it is of the view that there is an attack against it. This prompts the discharge of a complex mix of chemicals and hormones like cortisol, adrenaline, and norepinephrine. When they are released, they get our bodies ready for physical action. Consequently, the human body will first react simply by diverting blood to our muscles and second, it will stop the irrelevant bodily functions which could be digestion and others.

The cavemen received a rush of energy through the release of hormones like norepinephrine, cortisol, and adrenaline and this prepared him to either fight the lion or run away. That fast breathing and heart pounding sensation is as a result of adrenaline and also a boost of energy which empowers us to focus all our attention in order to respond swiftly to the present situation.

In our present world, we can still survive dangerous situations with the fight or flight mode. For instance, we can swiftly run away from a falling object or an oncoming vehicle. Also, it can alert us and empower us to slam the brakes when we are suddenly faced with someone running straight to the front of our car.

So, why worry about stress and why is it causing a lot of problem in our daily lives? Well, the moment we enter into a stressful state even in conditions that are not stressful, it becomes a problem. Our brain function is minimized when blood flow is channeled to the most crucial muscles that are needed to flee or fight. The implication is that we are unable to think properly which greatly hinders our ability to function well at home or at work. Remaining in a stressful condition for an extended time frame can greatly affect our health. A decreased libido, increased blood pressure levels, and sugar level can be as a result of increased cortisol level.

- **Flight-** So, when your body activates the flight mode, it causes us to avoid our stressors and remove ourselves from such a disturbing situation instead of dealing with it. This is a survival instinct which is the flight mode activated. Although it can save us in the face of danger, it can also cause a stressful situation to escalate and further increase our stress when we realize that the stress-causing factor is not going away and we have to face it.

- **Fight-** Sometimes, we feel stressed and this may increase our agitation and aggressiveness toward other people because our fight mode has been activated. Although this is helpful in case we want to ward off predators, but when this mode is activated in normal situations, it can affect our relationships negatively and ruin our reputations.

- **Freeze-** Most people are unaware of the third mode which is freeze. Yes, stress can cause our body to freeze. Stress can actually set the stage for "dysregulation" when the energy that was mobilized by the perceived threat is trapped in the nervous system causing us to freeze. Sometimes, this response shows when we breathe, shallow breath and holding of our breath are forms of freezing.

Common Signs and Symptoms of Stress

The ease with which stress creeps on you is what really makes it dangerous. You often get used to it as it starts feeling familiar- in some cases normal. You find it difficult noticing the extent to which stress is affecting your life and it gradually starts taking a toll on you. This explains why you need to be aware of the common signs and symptoms that may serve as a red flag of stress overload.

	Symptoms
Emotional Symptoms	<ul><li>Depression and unhappiness</li><li>Isolation and loneliness</li><li>Anxiety and agitation</li><li>Feeling like you're overwhelmed</li><li>Irritability, moodiness, and anger</li><li>Several other emotional and mental issues</li></ul>
Cognitive Symptoms	<ul><li>Constantly worrying</li><li>Unable to concentrate</li><li>Being negative</li><li>Memory issues</li><li>Poor judgment</li><li>Anxious and racing thoughts</li></ul>
Behavioral Symptoms	<ul><li>Withdrawing from other people</li></ul>

	▪ Adopting negative habits (pacing, nail biting, etc.)
	▪ Eating more or less
	▪ Trying to relax with alcohol, drugs, and cigarettes
	▪ Sleeping too little or too much
	▪ Neglecting responsibilities
Physical Symptoms	▪ Low sex drive Dizziness
	▪ Aches and pains
	▪ Pains in the chest and a heart rate that is a rapid
	▪ Frequent colds
	▪ Diarrhea or constipation

What Really Causes Stress?

What really causes stress for you may not cause stress for other people. So, you need to find what increases your stress level. Some of the causes of stress include:

40

Internal Stressors

- Negative self-talk
- Rigid thinking and lack of flexibility
- Pessimism
- Unrealistic expectations/perfectionism
- Unable to accept uncertainty
- Lack of flexibility, rigid thinking

External Stressors

- School work
- Children and family
- Financial issues
- Major life changes
- Issues in relationship
- Always too busy

Now you know some of the things that can cause stress for you. Take a look at the list of stressors and identify the ones that apply to you.

Based on the highly validated Holmes and Rahe Stress Scale, there are several stressful events that can contribute to illness in adults. Take a look at the top ten stressful life events:

- The loss of a spouse
- Divorce
- Separation of marriage
- Being imprisoned
- The death of a family member that was close
- Illness or injury
- Marriage
- Losing a job
- Reconciliation of marriage
- Retirement

Anxiety vs. Stress

Are you wondering if anxiety is different from stress? Well, you will definitely discover that both differ in several ways. Stress is as a result of the pressures we experience in life. As we aim to complete our daily tasks and deal with other life issues, undue pressure is placed on our body and mind causing the release of adrenalin and the persistence of the hormone will lead to blood pressure, depression, and other negative health effects. Check out the dissimilarities between stress and anxiety.

Anxiety	Stress
Anxiety is a feeling of fear which is often accompanied by the feelings of impending disaster. Also, the reason for this uneasiness is not often known and this adds to the distress you feel	Stress has to do with the way our minds and bodies react to anything that upsets the natural balance in life- like our response when we get threatened or frightened
factor The stress that continues even when the stressor is gone is anxiety	Stress is a by-product of an existing stressor or stress-causing

A major signal of increased stress level is when there is an escalation in your pulse rate and having a normal pulse rate does not mean that you're not stressed. In such cases, you should check for other symptoms like under-eating, decreased sexual desire, chronic fatigue, etc.

Anxiety is characterized by a feeling of unease and people often experience it when they encounter any stressful situation like a job interview, speaking in front of a large audience or being worried about an illness.

What really happens when we are Anxious and Stressed?

I guess you've heard of the flight or fight syndrome- our body's natural response to stress which causes our nervous system to prepare us to either run away or fight the challenging and dangerous situation. During the stone age when technology was not invented, we would be able to run as fast as our legs can run from an encroaching predator, however, fewer real-life challenges exist that can make us run that fast. In our modern world, our minds seem to process threat differently based on the feeling of being psychologically vulnerable, not liked, not good enough, not successful, not valued, etc. By learning to deal effectively with stress and anxiety, you can actually become less reactive to daily stressors that we encounter in life and you'll be able to enhance your general sense of well-being and generally feel calmer.

Depression/Unhappiness

Although we all feel sad from time to time because of certain events that might have taken place or things that we might have missed, there are people who experience a more intense feeling of unhappiness for an extended period of time (weeks, months and sometimes years) and sometimes they are unhappy for no apparent reason. Depression is a very serious health condition that impacts negatively on our physical and mental health. It affects the way you feel about yourself generally and this may lead to a loss of interest in work, life, hobbies and in the things you normally do. As a result of prolonged unhappiness, you may lack energy and experience difficulty in sleeping and in some cases you may sleep more than usual. Well, just like other forms of illness, unhappiness or depression can be treated and with the plan in this book, you will be empowered to break free from anxiety, stress, and unhappiness.

How to identify if you are depressed

First, you should understand that unhappiness is a product of depression because a person who is depressed is someone feeling sad, and miserable. How do you really know when you're depressed? well, if you're down, sad, lost interest in most usual activities, miserable most of the time for an extended period of time which usually exceeds two weeks and experience some other symptoms which you'll find below, then you're likely suffering from depression. One important thing to note though is that everyone will experience some of the symptoms of depression from time to time, however, it may not imply that we all are depressed. Also, it's not everyone that suffers from depression that will experience the common symptoms. The symptoms will serve as a guide or indicators of a possible case of depression but it cannot provide a diagnosis- you should visit your doctor.

Symptoms of Depression

	Symptoms
Feelings	<ul><li>Guilty</li><li>Overwhelmed</li><li>Frustrated</li><li>Unhappy</li><li>Sad</li><li>Irritable</li><li>Frustrated</li><li>Lack of confidence</li><li>Disappointed</li><li>Indecisive</li></ul>

	▪ Miserable
Behavior	▪ Not engaging in usually enjoyable activities
	▪ Not interested in going out any longer
	▪ Depending on sedatives and alcohol
	▪ getting things undone at work/school
	▪ Inability to concentrate
	▪ Withdrawing from close friends and family
Physical	▪ Sick and run down
	▪ Losing weight significantly
	▪ Always feeling tired
	▪ Having headaches and muscle pains
	▪ Experiencing sleep problems
	▪ Change or loss of appetite
Thoughts	▪ It's all my fault

- Life's not worth living
- I'm a failure
- Nothing good ever happens in my life
- People can do without me
- I'm worthless

SECTION II BREAKING THE CYCLE OF ANXIETY, STRESS, AND UNHAPPINESS

Chapter 3 Energy Consumers and Energy Providers

For years, you have continually demanded all manner of possible and impossible tasks from yourself. At home, at work, and in life you have continued to adapt to different things. You force and command yourself. Your social life has been so heavy that you find it hard to extricate yourself. All things are priorities – and everything seems to be important. At work, pressure continues to come from all corners as many things emerge that needs to be done at the same time. There are days when you can hardly find little spared time to eat something or even get to the bathroom other than work. While involving yourself too much in these pressure ravaged routines, you have lost touch with reality and your own needs begin to pay the price.

Daniel, a 43-year-old GP, went on a vacation in a crowded town in Bulgaria. Before leaving for this vacation, he had applied for a sick leave because he had discovered anxiety symptoms and was so stressed up. After things improve – the anxiety symptoms relaxed – he embarked on the vacation as planned. But on getting to Bulgaria, he soon realized that he is not enjoying himself. While eating, one of the mornings, he experienced something very unusual; there was a sense of fright and panic; the only thought he had was 'how can I move out from this place?' He only got himself again when he was alone in his room.

How did Daniel get so anxious and stressed out? Though after the first year of working, he realized that the job wasn't for him. He remained in the GP practice for another fifteen years and he is so proud of it. After turbulent years in high school, where he refused giving up because of his motto. He actually did this despite having a better judgment.

Can I Still Enjoy Myself?

Daniel was surprised he can no longer enjoy or find pleasure in doing what he often does, like making dinner with his family and going on vacations. Daniel enjoys nothing he does anymore. Not even a single bit. Daniel took a major step to list out things that give him energy and those that drew energy. He can only discover the areas in order to make changes in his anxious, stressed, and unhappy life.

Energy Consumers (stressors)		Energy Providers (boosters)	
Work-related	Personal	Work-related	Personal
Management	Shopping	Computer	Going to Coffee shop
Difficult Patients	Teenage Children	Making the right diagnosis	Going out for Dinner
Feeling detached	Cooking meals	Colleagues	Weekend Trip
Registering Patients for hospital	Visiting mother in nursing homes	A grateful patient	Visiting Family and friends.
Being on call at weekends	Doing menial		Playing a musical instrument

	jobs at home		
Not enough time for patients	Noisy neighbors		Reading an exciting book

Daniel changed his daily routine in a way that after a while, the list of energy providers or boosters increased considerably. He began to read more and even decided to be a specialist. He applied for another job in a nursing home (with the intention to quit the former) where he can work three days a week. With this new arrangement, he has more time for pleasure – like going for holidays and having a more social life. Daniel was able to intentionally reduce the stressed routine that caused him Unhappiness.

Count Your Blessings!

1. Itemize forty things you enjoy doing. They do not have to be expensive or big, think of things like; going to a museum, skating, going to dinner with

family, buying flowers, paying a visit to an old friend etc. little things that may remind you of what you previously did to enjoy yourself before the stress and anxiety crawled in.

2. Be in touch with your needs, desires, and wishes. Go somewhere quiet, sit still and feel your breathing in the belly. Say to yourself as you close your eye 'now I'm going to enjoy myself…ponder on the things you use to enjoy doing like; taking a photograph, walking-out or color painting. Look within yourself now, exhale the feeling it brings. Pleasant or unpleasant? How does this feeling affect your current mood? Is it enlightening? What is paramount in this exercise is to get in-touch with your inner feelings and help you make choices that will benefit you.

3. Just like we did above, make a list of activities that are energy consuming and wearing, and activities that are energy providing and nourishing. Follow the above framework.

Brain Well-Fed

After a career of twenty years at a University, Alison has not been working for almost two years due to Stress and unhappiness. Even at that, she has delayed her recovery. She has physical problems with no solution at hand. Not long, she was diagnosed of having irritable bowel syndrome, a contraction in the colon: she has pains in the left side of the abdomen, and suffers from cramps and constipation, alternating with periods of diarrhea. This syndrome can manifest due to mental strain and results in less energy because fewer nutrients from the food are absorbed.

Abdominal ache can actually be as a result of anxiety. That is why many people use this phrase 'my stomach turns when I think of the pile of the documents on my desk'. Or you hear 'all this things are indigestible'. Ultimately you get weighed down like there is a stone in your stomach. On the flip side, stomach abnormality also gives rise to a negative outlook. In this way, we end up in a vicious circle of powerlessness.

Anxiety and stress can have great influence on the digestive system. For example, when there is a sudden threat, blood leaves digestive tract and flows towards the skeletal muscles, so that the body is ready to flee or fight. Severe stress leads to disrupted digestion. Stress inhibits the wavelike, contracting movements (peristalsis) of the intestines so that the food can travel down. Stress influences digestion in another way in that it decreases or increases the manufacturing of gastric fluid which ultimately harms the mucous membrane of the abdomen.

Healthy Fuel

Reducing stress is indeed an essential remedy, but incorporating a balanced and nutritious diet is equally imperative. It is crucial to evaluate the nutritional value of the food you consume, particularly the composition of fats and sugars. Surprisingly, fish fats offer numerous health benefits to the human body compared to other animal fats. The consumption of fatty fish not only enhances brain function but also reduces the likelihood of cardiovascular disease, depression, and burnout. Optimal choices for improved health include salmon, tuna, herring, sardines, mackerel, trout, and anchovies. Additionally, plant-based sources such as walnuts, soy products, linseed, rapeseed, pumpkin seed, and hemp seed also contain healthier fats.

Taking a moment to reflect on your daily meals is essential. Are your meals well-balanced and nutritious? Consider the following key factors:

- Stop smoking gradually, experiment with a smoke-free day now and again, and determine for yourself the date you will give up smoking altogether. Ask your doctor for advice, read something about giving up smoking or follow a workshop in how to stop smoking.
- Limit your alcohol intake to four glasses per week.
- For one month give up drinking coffee and see how that feels.
- Avoid working breakfasts or working lunches. They are not conducive to good digestion because you are more stressed. The digestion will not get going

properly, and you leave the table feeling bloated. With the nasty result that your energy has also gone out the window for the rest of the day. At least once a week have lunch on your own.

- Try out foods you are not yet familiar with; buy a new cookery book and prepare a new dish every week.

- Don't eat refined sugar, but choose honey or pureed fruits when you want something sweet.

Do you already suffer from stomach complaints? Try this:

- Replace white flour, pasta and white bread with wholegrain products.

- Make yourself some vegetable juices. For instance, mix three parts of carrot juice with one part of cabbage juice (it tastes better than it sounds).

- Aloe Vera juice helps to heal the mucous membrane of the stomach. Dilute the juice (you need 99% pure juice for this) with as much water as juice.

- Drink a few cups of mint tea after your meals.

- Sprinkle milled seeds over your muesli or food, like sunflower seeds, sesame seeds, and linseed or hemp seed. Add some oat flakes to the muesli; this too helps to heal the stomach lining.

- Test yourself for allergies to dairy products, and to products containing wheat or gluten by not eating these for a few weeks. Good alternatives can be found in health food shops. How does your body react when you take dairy and wheat or gluten products again one by one? When it does not feel right, omit them from your diet. (Source: The Times Energy Plan 2001.)

Empty the Mind to Sleep

Finding it hard to fall asleep? Are you counting each hour of the night the striking of the church clock? Do you find yourself awake in the middle of the night and unable to sleep again? Or do you wake up very early, like five o'clock in the morning? Sleep disorders are common with depression, RSI, chronic pain, and burnout. Insomnia often leads to tossing and turning in bed, and to worrying and fretting. Some people complain that they seem incapable of stopping their thoughts. When you don't sleep well at night you may worry about this during the day. You fear that through lack of sleep you won't be able to work so well and are more likely to make mistakes. Some people feel tired when they wake up. Below some recommendations are given, partly taken from The Times Energy Plan (2001).

Rest and Order

The foundation for a restful night's sleep commences in the morning. Instead of lingering in bed due to a restless night, maintain your regular wake-up time. If possible, consider rising five or ten minutes earlier to allow for a brief meditation or relaxation practice. Throughout the day, incorporate three to five relaxation exercises, ensuring to include one just before bedtime.

Engaging in physically demanding activities three times a week is recommended. Whether it's sports, fitness workouts, jogging, roller-skating, or swimming, prioritize these exercises during the daytime rather than in the evening.

Exerting yourself before bed can leave you wide-awake, hindering your ability to fall asleep. It is crucial to dedicate at least one part of the day to relaxation, fostering a peaceful state of mind.

Half hour before going to bed, so watching a thriller just before bedtime is not such a good idea either. There will be tension in your body, and it will be impossible to fall asleep quietly.

Watch out for light in your bedroom, because light influences your biological clock. Make sure you have good curtains that block out the light. Bright light in the morning or in the middle of the night upsets your biological clock. Are you suffering more from insomnia in winter – and do you always feel somewhat down in January? Perhaps you are sensitive to winter depressions. A little bit of light works wonders. Make sure you have bright fluorescent lights over your workstation, and regularly going for sessions on a sunbed also helps.

Is your bedroom comfortable and not too hot? Do you have1 a good mattress less than ten years old? Are you turning the mattress once in a while? Can you open a window at night? And even though you might be able to sleep anywhere, in any position – for instance on an airplane – a good climate and atmosphere in the bedroom are important. How are the noise levels in your bedroom? The rhythmic sound of raindrops falling on the tent, or the murmurs of a waterfall, can help you to fall asleep. Accelerating vehicles, low flying aircraft, rows or loud music from the neighbors can prevent you from falling asleep, and make you feel vulnerable when these sounds suddenly wake you up. Try to sleep in a quiet room in the house.

Heavy food can disturb your sleep. On the other hand, some foods can make you tired, for instance, a meal that is rich in fats and low in carbohydrates. People who experience 'restless legs' at night can take some extra magnesium in their food. For instance, you could eat dried figs, which are extremely rich in magnesium, before going to bed. Rye bread, nuts, and seeds, broccoli and kale are good sources of magnesium. Doing some stretches before going to bed can also help against the nervous twitching of the legs.

A Hot Bath

Take a hot bath two hours before you go to bed. You could add some chamomile. Stir two spoons of chamomile in boiling water and let it stand for ten minutes. Pour this through a sieve into the bath. Try a footbath for a change. Put down two big bowls or buckets, one with hot water, the other with cold water. Put your feet for three or four minutes in the hot water and then for thirty seconds in the cold water. Repeat four times. The smell of lavender is also relaxing. Burn some lavender oil in an oil burner in your bedroom before going to bed. Or sleep with a lavender bag under your pillow.

Empty Your Mind

A lot of people worry. The problems at work stay with them when they get home. By doing a meditation exercise early in the evening you will prevent worrying. Do a short relaxation exercise (see day 12), keep your eyes lightly closed and bring your attention to the breathing. Inhale and exhale thrice. Observe your mind to find out what is happening. Don't suppress it, but just notice it: it is allowed to be there. Afterward, write down everything you noticed. All the thoughts that are running riot: your plans, snippets of thoughts, memories. You will notice that it is much easier now to let go of everything.

Herbal Nightcap

There are various herbal teas available that promote sleep. You could also mix a relaxing or sleep-inducing tea yourself. Take three types of tea from the following list: hops, valerian, chamomile flowers, green mint, hawthorn berries, St. John's Wort, passion flower, kava, and lemon balm. Try to avoid sleeping pills as much as possible. Two American studies involving a million patients showed that taking sleeping tablets on a daily basis is as detrimental to our health as smoking one to two packets of cigarettes a day. The risk of dying from damaged respiratory organs is six to eight times higher. Other nasty side effects of sleeping pills can be that you enter into a kind of coma, from which you wake when the effect of the tablets has worn off. So there is no natural sleep, and often it becomes impossible to fall asleep without these pills. Or you wake up with some kind of hangover because the sleep was not natural.

Counting Sheep new Style

When you are really lying awake, try to focus on something else. Don't continue to have thoughts like: I can't sleep! When we were young we were told to count sheep; now you can do a meditation exercise. Bring your breathing down into your belly, and breath-in, then count one and breathe out. At the next in-breath count two, and breathe out. When breathing in again count one, and breathe out, and on the next in-breath count two, and breathe out, and so on.

Don't reward yourself for being awake. Don't read interesting books, or make cups of tea for yourself with a treat. You will notice that when you do something nice you will only wake up more often and stay awake longer. When, on the contrary, you do something boring like copying the telephone directory, your sleeplessness will soon vanish.

Even if you are lying awake for hours: don't get up. In this way, your body will still get a chance to rest. It won't do you any harm not to sleep; perhaps you won't sleep well for several nights. But you will notice that eventually, you will sleep very deeply for a few nights in a row. Usually, the balance restores by itself. Trust in that.

Chapter 4 Positive Thoughts

When management consultant Josh Klang was in the process of splitting up one of the largest solicitors' firms in the Netherlands, he described in 'Dutch Diary', his column in one of the leading Dutch newspapers, how he handled his emotions. He needed to get all parties concerned to agree on a course of action and he often felt like 'the only lamppost in a street with seventy dogs'. In order to be able to deal with that Josh applies three strategies. One evening every week he practices yoga, where he can completely relax. 'I must admit it does look rather comical, five men on a yoga mat.' Secondly he takes a foreign colleague, Raj Raitheta of Versatel, as an example.

According to Raitheta, Versatel's strength actually lies in positive thinking. The third strategy is to present the new office management with a survival package, which consists of rose-tinted spectacles, a box of pep pills, a boxing ball to work off stress, and a cuddly toy animal for lonely moments.

Rational Emotive Therapy

Putting on rose-colored spectacles happens when you think positively. You can achieve this by practicing extensively in the Rational Emotive Therapy (RET). The premise of this method is that people are not troubled by actual experiences but by the way they interpret these experiences. The American RET psychologist Albert Ellis says: 'We often suffer unnecessarily because our heads are full of wrong ideas about life. When one counteracts these rationally, all negative emotions will disappear.'

But beware: thinking positively cannot solve all problems. It is not a way to make right what is wrong. RET does not offer a real solution for a political prisoner who has been tortured, or for someone with a life-threatening illness. RET is an extremely beneficial remedy in situations that can be looked at from a different angle. It deals with the subtle distinction between subjectivity and objectivity.

Ask yourself the question: would everyone else who has these experiences also suffer from them? If the answer is yes, then RET is only of limited value. But if you think that it is not fair that something is happening to you, then RET can help to challenge this thought.

Ask yourself the question: is it fairer when this would happen to someone else? Why is it not allowed to happen to you specifically? In this way, you could gradually analyze and invalidate your own (negative) thought patterns.

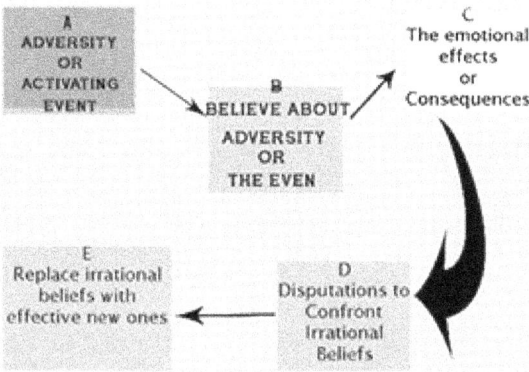

A		C
ADVERSITY OR ACTIVATING EVENT	B BELIEVE ABOUT ADVERSITY OR THE EVEN	The emotional effects or Consequences
E Replace irrational beliefs with effective new ones	D Disputations to Confront Irrational Beliefs	

At what Point does the Rose-tinted glasses really work?

How do you know whether RET is a suitable approach to your problems? As a rule, you can go from the premise that you can view the problem from a different perspective.

Take for instance Peter, a teacher of German in a grammar school, who got burnt out because of the reorganization of the educational system for secondary schools. Is it more beneficial for him to continue to dismiss the innovations in the education system and to wage a political battle? Or would he be better off to take a closer look at his feelings in order to change them? RET could be helpful here: for there are also teachers who feel happy with the new system. They see it as a challenge and they enjoy their new role as coach and guide.

How to use those rose-tinted spectacles can be illustrated with the following example.

The rose-tinted spectacles: the ABCDE model of Rational Emotive Therapy

The ABCDE model consists of five steps. First of all, you describe the situation that gives you an unpleasant feeling. That situation is A; the negative feeling or consequences of your emotion is C. The negative feeling arises because of how you look at (your beliefs about) the situation. This is B. The thoughts in B can be challenged by asking yourself the following four questions:

1. Is this true; what are the facts?

2. Will I, by thinking in this way, reach my goal?

3. Do I not get unnecessarily into conflict with myself?

4. Or with someone else?

A = Activating event or problematic situation.

B = Belief or irrational thought.

C = Consequence: that unhelpful behavior.

D = Discussion with yourself: challenging the irrational thoughts.

E = Effect, the description of how you want to feel in the situation

An example of putting on rose-tinted spectacles

In this instance, the activating event that makes Peter feel unpleasant is the introduction of new educational policies.

Belief about these policies, the irrational thoughts

1. I don't do justice to my students because I can no longer teach them in appropriate ways. Therefore they will fail their exams.

2. I can't deal with this, I no longer have any control, and I am powerless.

3. It would be better if I pulled out and let go of my engagement and involvement.

4. I notice that students lose their way. If I could have taught them in the old way, I would have been able to save them.

5. I don't do justice to myself by forcing myself to teach in this new way.

The consequence, the unpleasant irritation feeling, fear, and sadness.

Discussion: challenging irrational thoughts, what can be said about them?

1. It is not true that everyone is a victim. One category of students are not doing so well, but I have talked this through with the school principal and he will take appropriate measures.

2. Is that so? I see that my colleague who has been coached is well able to deal with the new system. Perhaps I should go and get some coaching too.

3. Would I reach my goal – teaching in a pleasant manner – by doing so? No, not at all. It would be better if I set my own goals and try to achieve them with the help of a coach. Even at my age, there is still a lot that can be learned. Although I regret that I can no longer work in the old way.

4. I am not sure if I could have saved them, and by presuming that I could, I take on a lot of responsibility. I also have colleagues here. However, it is my responsibility to give it my best in class. I am not responsible if a student falls by the wayside.

5. Is it true that I do myself an injustice? I only do so if I insist on sticking to my old methods of teaching while nowadays a new skill is being asked of me. Others have found joy in that, why would that not be possible for me?

The effect, how I want to feel calm, in control of my own feelings.

Practicing Positive Thinking

Peter has decided to go for coaching and to adapt his style of teaching to the demands of the new educational system. He feels a lot more at ease and is better able to sleep. The feelings of being powerless have disappeared. He has shared his feelings of powerlessness with his colleagues and they now offer more support. For they definitely do not want to lose him; they appreciate him greatly as a colleague and as a teacher. Now, look at your own stress diary. Which situation would benefit from a RET? From now on make a daily RET analysis of such a situation according to the diagram below.

The interpretation of the ABCDE model diagram of the RET

74

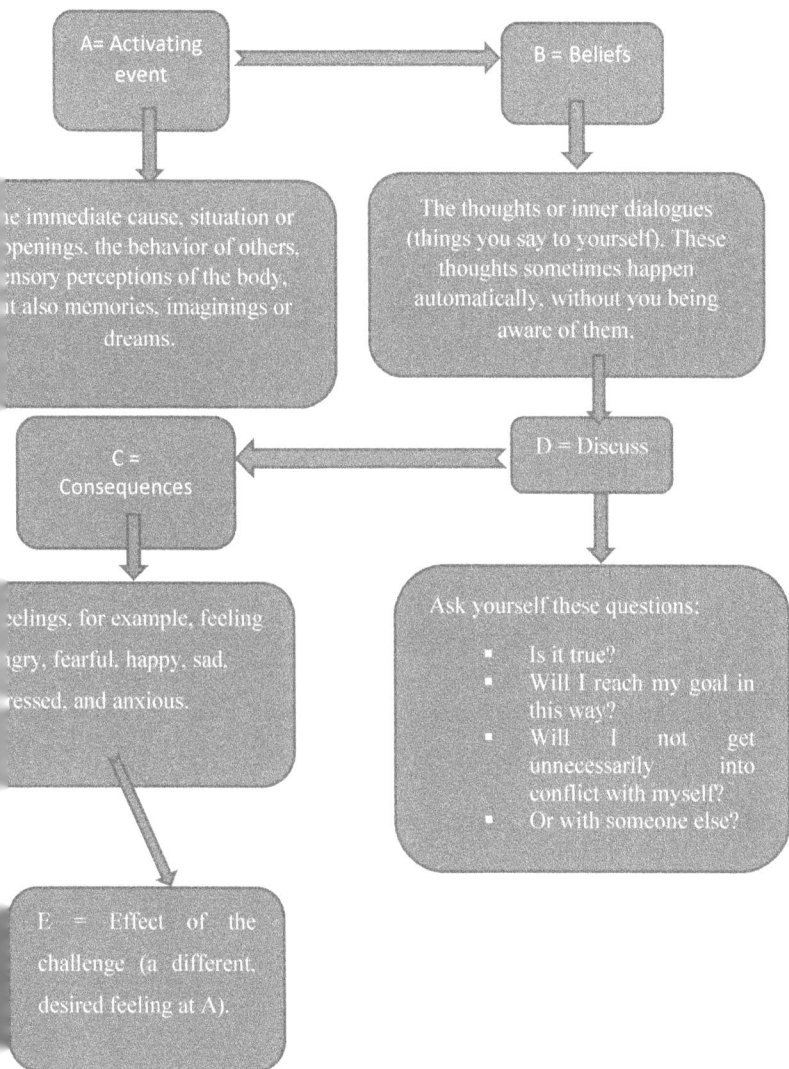

```
┌─────────────────────┐                              ┌─────────────────────┐
│  A= Activating      │◄────────────────────────────►│  B = Beliefs        │
│  event              │                              │                     │
└─────────────────────┘                              └─────────────────────┘
         │                                                      │
         ▼                                                      ▼
┌─────────────────────┐                    ┌──────────────────────────────────┐
│ ...e immediate      │                    │ The thoughts or inner dialogues   │
│ cause, situation or │                    │ (things you say to yourself). These│
│ ...penings, the     │                    │ thoughts sometimes happen          │
│ behavior of others, │                    │ automatically, without you being   │
│ ...nsory perceptions│                    │ aware of them.                     │
│ of the body,        │                    │                                    │
│ ...t also memories, │                    └──────────────────────────────────┘
│ imaginings or       │                                      │
│ dreams.             │                                      ▼
└─────────────────────┘          ┌─────────────────────┐   ┌─────────────────────┐
                                 │  C =                │◄──│  D = Discuss        │
                                 │  Consequences       │   └─────────────────────┘
                                 └─────────────────────┘             │
                                          │                          ▼
                                          ▼
┌─────────────────────┐          ┌──────────────────────────────────┐
│ ...elings, for      │          │ Ask yourself these questions:     │
│ example, feeling    │          │    ▪ Is it true?                  │
│ ...gry, fearful,    │          │    ▪ Will I reach my goal in      │
│ happy, sad,         │          │      this way?                    │
│ ...essed, and       │          │    ▪ Will I not get               │
│ anxious.            │          │      unnecessarily into           │
│                     │          │      conflict with myself?        │
└─────────────────────┘          │    ▪ Or with someone else?        │
         │                       └──────────────────────────────────┘
         ▼
┌─────────────────────┐
│ E = Effect of the   │
│ challenge (a        │
│ different,          │
│ desired feeling at  │
│ A).                 │
└─────────────────────┘
```

Chapter 5 Set Realizable Daily Targets

In most mental training the participants are asked to set goals for themselves. When you feel down or depressed, this is very difficult. You feel helpless and are inclined to throw in the towel. You start having a tunnel vision; a situation where you only observe the things that are going in the wrong direction. Body and mind work together, so when you think like this, you will also feel heavy and tired physically. You cannot be bothered to continue.

We have already seen that it may be helpful to learn to think in a different way. And you can use the ABCDE model to do this. But you can also learn to listen better to yourself. Make use of the knowledge you have about what is good for you. What do you think would benefit you most? In what situations do you feel most comfortable and are you at your best?

Trust Your Intuition

Use your self-knowledge for a conscious thinking strategy. Professor Damasio, an expert in neurobiology, shows with an example taken from worker bees how body and mind collaborate. In a field with flowers in many different colors worker bees know exactly on which flowers to land in order to obtain the much-desired honey. In doing so they make use of knowledge, the theory of probabilities and a conscious thinking strategy:

- Flowers from which they expect a good yield get preferential treatment over flowers from which they expect less profit (a lot of honey over little honey);

- Flowers that are low risk are preferred over flowers that are high risk (no bee-eaters present on the flower).

The simple, automatic brain of the worker bee can in this way carry out the complicated task of gathering food. Damasio compares this to human intuition, which sometimes works in a similar way, bypassing the conscious brain. Intuitively you make choices. Intuition is made up of knowledge, the theory of probabilities and a conscious thinking strategy, just as with the worker bees. What Damasio means is that intuitively we know what is good for us. And also that intuition follows indeed a rationale that we ourselves are not aware of.

Repair the Contact

When we arrive in the tunnel that leads to stress, our vision becomes extremely narrow. The contact between body and mind has been lost or disturbed. Often this has been going on for a long time already, and that is also the reason why, for example, you keep on working in a job that is not good for you. You have disconnected from your own intuition through long-term habituation to an unpleasant situation. Knowing what is right for you is a process. When you are feeling well you crave food that is right for you. When you are engaged in sports, you feel like taking vitamin C and eating grain products such as pasta. Pregnant women often have a craving for herring; the fatty oil in this fish is extremely beneficial for the formation of the brain of their baby. So we begin by becoming aware of the interaction between body and mind. When you imagine going for a bicycle trip, does that feel right? Or do you already feel nauseous when you are just thinking about it? When you imagine your colleagues coming to visit you, do you feel energetic or does it make you feel heavy-hearted and anxious? Become aware of what your own preferences are and trust that these preferences will serve you well in your survival, in your looking after yourself.

Keep Your Goals in Sight

The outcome of the Olympic hockey championships was determined by a single crucial penalty. As Stephan Veen prepared to take the shot, his mind became plagued with negative thoughts. Despite being recognized as the world's finest hockey player, the weight of the situation bore down on him: "I've already scored three goals, this is my final game of the competition, it's a matter of gold or silver; this won't work." But in a mere two seconds, those thoughts vanished.

Once again, clarity dawned upon him, reminding him of his task: to focus on executing one successful penalty and envisioning the accompanying emotions. Yet, it felt perpetually unattainable. Fortunately, Stephan Veen employed a powerful technique: visualization. The hockey team had undergone mental training, during which the psychologist instructed them to imagine a triumphant experience from their past, emphasizing the importance of embracing the associated emotions.

In mental training, it is essential to establish clear goals and articulate them. The mind possesses a natural inclination towards visual imagery, which can be harnessed to profoundly influence one's emotions. For instance, if facing a job interview, it is beneficial to imagine a previous successful interview. Similarly, when entering a negotiation with a boss, visualizing a past instance where a 10% salary increase was achieved proves advantageous. The astonishing words spoken on the day of receiving the offer left her astounded. She entered her room, fighting back tears, but as the day wore on, the floodgates opened, and she found herself overwhelmed with a torrent of emotions, for she was deeply moved.

Stephen Veen admits that it is difficult to visualize the positive feeling together with the successful image. At first, he also experienced negative feelings. But the more you practice, the better you will be able to visualize a positive image. Stephan Veen imagined a successful penalty. This is how he succeeded to utilize the last and decisive penalty cold-bloodedly so that the Dutch team went home with a gold medal. If you want to apply his experience in your situation it means that you have to set goals for yourself. You can support this by remembering the times you succeeded in reaching another goal; an experience of having been successful. It does not matter what the goal was, whether it was getting your swimming diploma or your driving license; what is important is that you succeeded. When you can imagine a successful experience, setting yourself goals will be your next step.

The Inner Source

This exercise may help you to discover or access your own goals. It is a visualization exercise. Ask somebody else to read the practice to you slowly. It begins with a short relaxation exercise. Practice some stretches in order to get your body relaxed. Let your focus be completely on your breathing. Then on the in-breath, you expand your belly and on the out-breath, you pull your belly in a little bit. Put a hand on your belly and feel how your hand rises up when the belly expands and how it falls back again on the out-breath. Close your eyes. Let go of all worries and thoughts. Imagine you are in a place where you feel totally safe and secure. This can be at home, on a walk in the woods or in the sun on the beach.

Then you start Your Journey.

You walk on a long road leading to a gate. When you get to the gate you really look at it. You take in the shape and the color; you smell the material the gate is made from. You look for the handle and you find it. Very carefully you open the gate. Slowly you step through it and you close the gate behind you.

You have ended up in an unkempt garden, with tall grasses. You see poppies in flower, and big, mature fruit trees. Full of curiosity you keep going and you discover a flight of stairs going down. At every step that you go down on those stairs, you feel more and more relaxed. Say to yourself with every step going down: 'deeper and deeper.' After the last step, you get to a meadow. You walk for ten steps and then you arrive at the edge of a forest. You walk on the soft earth underneath the trees and breathe in the fresh air of the greenery and the moss. You hear birdsong.

Eventually, you feel it takes too long. Is there no end to this forest? You no longer recognize sounds; the crunching of the twigs underfoot and the flashing shadows make you anxious. You start to walk faster and you give a sigh of relief when you arrive at a clearing.

As you stand there, a profound sense of awe washes over you. Before your eyes lies an enchanting sanctuary, emanating an unparalleled aura of tranquility and serenity. Step by step, you venture deeper into the heart of this ethereal place. And there, at the center, a lively spring reveals itself. Seating yourself beside its gentle waters, you fix your gaze upon its shimmering surface, as if it holds the secrets to your innermost desires. With unwavering focus, you attune your senses to the spring's murmurs, for it seems to carry a profound message meant exclusively for you. Absorbed in the moment, you receive its words with utmost care, cherishing the profound wisdom they impart.

After a while, you rise from your serene spot, ready to embark on your homeward journey. The forest path now appears considerably shorter, as if time itself has granted you swifter passage. As you reach the meadow, your feet guide you toward the stone staircase. But before ascending the steps, you pause and cast one final glance back at the spring, the lingering echoes of its message resonating within you. With a sense of deep reflection, you ascend the steps, gradually returning to the gate. As you stand before it, you take hold of the latch, ensuring its secure closure, safeguarding the sanctuary from prying eyes.

Now, let the path before the gate guide you back to your present reality. Take as much time as you need to reorient yourself, fully embracing the space you inhabit once again. Slowly, open your eyes, allowing the sights around you to reacquaint you with the familiar. If desired, indulge in a refreshing stretch, grounding yourself in the here and now.

Then think back to the journey and try to answer the following questions:

- What did the spring look like?
- Was it a powerful gushing of water or just a trickle?
- What was the message?
- What does the spring say about your needs, your wishes, and your desires?
- What is really a necessity, and what is more like a wish?

When you have charted your needs, wishes and desires, try to set three goals that match your inner needs, wishes and desires.

What are Your Goals?

Spend five minutes every day for the mental training to reach your goals. Bring one successful experience in reaching your goal to mind, and keep focusing on it. Arouse the accompanying feeling. What positive thought about yourself goes along with that image and that feeling? I can do it or I am successful? Then imagine the new goal together with the feeling of the positive experience and the positive thought.

Make a mantra out of this positive evaluation of yourself, and say this mantra in your mind. In difficult situations or perhaps specifically at a peaceful moment, think of yourself while you say: I am happy or the sun is shining again. The mantra can also consist of naming your core quality.

SECTION III THE POWER OF MEDITATION

Chapter 6 Meditation and Deep Breathing for Anxiety Relief

Have you ever wondered why two people perform the same job with the same working conditions and one is overwhelmed, hates his job and completely stressed while the other person is happy and handles the job for the day with ease?. Well according to the latest studies in neuroscience, it has been discovered that stress-related behaviors are really hard-wired into the human brain- they are actually less about the environment and more about we react to it individually.

One of the crucial aspects of the 30 days plan is to practice meditation and deep breathing. For thousands of years, people have practiced meditation and its benefits have no doubt been enjoyed by many. I'm sure you must have heard about meditation before or someone might have suggested it to you. Well, if you're serious about dealing with anxiety and stress and you want to enjoy a happier life, you need to regularly practice meditation and deep breathing.

Deep Breathing

Most of us tend to overlook deep breathing while others tend not to give it much thought, but there are great benefits from deep breathing. One of the steps to breaking the cycle of stress is to do deep breathing regularly. When you practice deep breathing, it enables oxygen to enter our lungs causing more oxygen to be sent to our heart. Consequently, it heightens our cardiovascular capacity and also the amount of oxygen that will be delivered to our cells.

Practicing deep breathing enables our cells to continue in an aerobic state and this state encourages burning of fat instead of energy stores of glycogen. Additionally, it helps us to relax, detox and provides us with mental clarity. Deep breathing also moves our body out of the control of the sympathetic nervous system and takes us into the parasympathetic mode which is a healthier and calmer state in terms of biochemical balance and general well-being.

When our stress hormone such as cortisol is curbed, it preserves our immune function and properly regulates blood pressure and heart rate. Also, when you practice deep breathing for relaxation, you will be able to influence gene expression that's related to oxidative stress, inflammation, and cellular metabolism. I must encourage you to practice deep breathing for a longer time because the longer you practice it the more significant the benefits will be for any particular condition. So, are you wondering how you can practice deep breathing? The steps below will assist you in practicing deep breathing:

- Find a comfortable position and place your hands on your stomach and chest.

- In order to maximize oxygen intake, you need to learn belly breathing (breathing from your abdomen) instead of your chest. Simply focus on your breathing until you can feel your stomach as it rises and falls more significantly than your chest with every inhalation and exhalation.

- Inhale via your nose, then hold your breath at least for some seconds before leasing the air through your mouth. Take note that when exhaling, you should spend twice the time it took you to inhale. You can use the popular suggestion (4:7:8 pattern), 4 seconds to inhale, 7 seconds to hold the breath and 8 seconds to exhale. While you breathe, you should let go of other disturbing thoughts and pressures at home or work.

- Now, as you continue to do this, you can add images to your breathing. You can imagine the air you're breathing spreading calmness and relaxation all through your body.

- When exhaling, try to visualize your breath whooshing away every form of tension and stress in your body. Now, practice the suggested 4-8 seconds deep breathing cycles again for about 10 minutes or until you feel less stressed and relaxed.

If you've not been practicing deep breathing, then you should make it part of your goals because it's part of the 30-

plan to break the cycle of stress and anxiety. It's really simple and does not need much time. You can practice it anywhere provided you can shut out all the noise and distractions and focus for few minutes.

The Power of Meditation

In breaking the cycle of anxiety, stress, and unhappiness, you need to embrace meditation which is one of the most important steps in this book. I'll suggest you pay good attention to this chapter since it's one effective way to break the cycle of sadness in your life without taking drugs. In order to understand the effect of meditation, you need to understand how anxiety alters the human brain. Anxiety does not just make you feel unhappy and sad, it actually alters the structure and function of your brain. It can decrease the size of the hippocampus which is the part of the human brain that is considered to be the seat of memory. Also, it increases the size of the part of the human brain that's responsible for the fear response (amygdala) and this makes you even more fearful and anxious. The combination of fear, anxiety, and stress is a deadly one and it will trigger the release of stress hormones leading to imbalances in neurotransmitters- chemicals used by brain cells in communicating with each other.

So how does Meditation Help?

Although it has been known for thousands of years that meditation can help the body to relax, there are other things that it can do for you. Just like anxiety, meditation can change both the structure and function of your brain positively. The regular practice of meditation will not only reduce the symptoms of anxiety, it can also reverse most of the damages caused by anxiety. These changes can be tracked with the help of neuroimaging techniques. John Hopkins University researchers assessed more than 18,000 mindfulness meditation studies in a bid to determine its most effective uses and it was discovered that the most important use of meditation is the relief of anxiety. (4)

There are also several other studies which confirm that meditation helps to deal with mental disorders and this includes panic disorder, anxiety disorder, generalized anxiety disorder, depression, binge eating disorder, addictions, attention deficit, agoraphobia, social anxiety, bipolar disorder and hyperactivity disorder.

Chapter 7 How Meditation Breaks the Cycle of Anxiety

You don't need any methods to get rid of the wrong ideas you have about yourself. All you have to do is stop believing them. The best way to do this is to replace them with ideas that more accurately reflect the real state of affairs. - Annamalai Swami

Let's take a look at various ways meditation can help improve your mental well-being and your brain.

Meditation Disrupts Anxious Thought Patterns

One of the major ways that meditation can help deal with anxiety is by disrupting negative thought patterns. If you're suffering from anxiety, you will attest to the fact that racing thoughts are responsible for establishing the vicious cycle of anxiety and worry and meditation is very effective in breaking the cycle of obsessive negative thinking. It can greatly reduce rumination even in people experiencing lifelong mood disorders. Meditation reduces the urge to worry and enforces your control over random unwanted thoughts.

It can also change the manner your brain responds to stress. Because of the strong pathway that habits establish through constant repetition, they are quite difficult to break. There are also few habits that are more difficult to break than negative patterns of self-talk. It's estimated that most of us harbor about 50,000 thoughts on a daily basis and surprisingly, majority of these thoughts are negative. Well, the good news is that our brain's capacity to change (neuroplasticity) is endless. When you practice meditation, it can train you to view most of your thoughts differently. You will develop the mental capacity to identify and stop "mental time travel" (when we worry about the future and also ponder the past. Rather than follow a worrying thought down the path of every possible negative result, you will learn to identify it for what it is- just a thought- and let go of the thought. It gets much better when you create a new thought pattern because you will be training your brain not to be too anxious.

Meditation Helps to Balance Brain Chemicals

Actually, the cause of anxiety is still not very precise. Its risk factors include emotional trauma, personality type, and your genes too. It is also believed that one of the things that can lead to anxiety is an imbalance of brain chemicals due to prolonged or severe stress. Meditation can also help remedy such situation because it can restore an optimal balance of neurotransmitters. It increases the level of a neurotransmitter that is necessary for feeling relaxed and happy- gamma-aminobutyric acid (GABA). When you feel overwhelmed, anxious and easily overstimulated, then these are signals of low level of GABA.

When you practice meditation, it will help to lift your mood by increasing the levels of serotonin in your body. Serotonin is also a neurotransmitter that is essential for feeling happy. The excess of cortisol in the body can lead to increase in stress because cortisol contributes to depression, memory loss, anxiety and sleep disorders, however, meditation can help to reduce cortisol.

Meditation Helps to Reduce Brain Inflammation

The chemical messengers that regulate the body's immune response are known as cytokines and the increased levels of cytokines are responsible for chronic inflammation which includes the inflammation of the brain. It's associated with depression, anxiety, and other mood disorders. Not only does meditation reduce inflammation, it also alters the expression of pro-inflammatory genes. Although we could think that changing genes will require a long time and process, however, reasonable changes can even be identified after as little as eight hours of meditation.

Builds a Healthier Brain

There is an unusual increase in the volume of the hippocampus, the amount of gray matter and the thickness of the cortex in people who practice meditation regularly. This is because meditation can help to build a healthier and bigger brain. At the same time, it decreases the size of the amygdala which is the area of the human brain that's associated with fear, stress, and anxiety and makes it less reactive. Meditation helps to increase the blood flow to the brain, it improves neural connections between different areas of the brain and also enhances the neuroplasticity. In fact, it can actually future-proof you against Alzheimer's disease and age-related mental decline.

Meditation for the Relief of Anxiety

It's believed that the best style of meditation for the relief of anxiety is mindfulness meditation. According to research, it has been found to be more helpful especially for anxiety than other forms of meditation. Because it's quite easy to do, it is also considered as the best beginner's meditation. It is effective and needs no special training to start, in fact, most people who frequently experience anxiety choose this kind of meditation while others engaged in high-stress occupations like silicon valley entrepreneurs, Wall Street brokers depend on it to prevent burn out and retain their mental edge. Also, you need to know that the US Marines make use of mindfulness to help reduce the overall on-the-job stress they encounter, improve their performance and also minimize any effects of post-traumatic stress.

Practicing Mindfulness Meditation

Generally, mindfulness meditation doesn't require a lot of time and a reasonable goal can be just 10 minutes of meditation daily. You don't need to be perfect, you can even start with as little as two minutes each day so that you can build the habit. Then gradually increase the duration as you get used to it. The first step is to start with breathing mindfulness meditation. Remember, I previously talked about deep breathing which will help in relieving stress, well this is a bit different. You have to practice this frequently until you're able to train your brain to stop jumping around and instead focus on the present. Take a look at the steps:

- Having closed your eyes, take a sitting position
- Take in your normal breaths and just observe your breath
- To keep other thoughts at bay, you can simply say "breathing in, breathing out" to yourself

- In the event that you observe a random thought, simply tag it as a "thought," then bring your attention gently back to your breath.

Several people that are new to meditation are erroneously of the view that when they have other thoughts during meditation that they have failed but that's not true.

Note that your goal is not having any thoughts at all but it is simply to notice any thoughts when they come up and to gently brush the thoughts aside.

This is why most people abandon meditation since they are of the view that they would not be able to quieten their thoughts and since they can't silence their thoughts they are not practicing meditation the right way. However, you can also practice guided meditation for anxiety. During such practice, you are usually not alone, rather, you practice along with a teacher that is experienced who will help guide you into a relaxed meditative state. A guided meditation is any meditation that is practiced with the assistance of a guide. This could either be in person or online and it could also be a digital download. The good thing about guided meditation is that you can find free guided meditations online.

Meditations to Help Banish Stress

I have compiled 8 meditation strategies to banish stress from your brain. Remember, you need to have some discipline to be able to develop a positive habit. So you have to start practicing and it does not have to be for hours, you can actually finish in a matter of minutes.

Meditation to Start Your Day

The way you start your day, right after waking up can really frame your entire day. So, you should endeavor to maintain a peaceful mindset which will also provide a positive outlook for you the entire day.

- Wake up at least 15 minutes before your usual time
- Search for a quiet where you can sit, then shut your eyes.

- Tilt your head forward toward your heart then follow your breathing and feel each breath open your heart and inject live into your brain with oxygen

- Feel immense gratitude for a new day with people you love

- Look forward to a rewarding day and say to yourself "you'll be peaceful and positive no matter what happens.

Identifying What Stresses you

Sometimes, you might find it difficult to avoid stress especially when you don't know what triggers it in the first place. This strategy enables you to take note of the stressors that you experience and you will be able to focus your attitude on them. This way, your control over your feelings and thoughts will greatly increase.

- First, acknowledge the things that prompts the negative thoughts in you

- Avoid changing the triggers but just observe them.

- Remember, your thoughts are powerless when you don't believe them, so simply tell yourself "this feelings or thoughts exists in me but not in reality." Simply declare; "What I see is peace and not my current issues." Your focus needs to be shifted to a peaceful alternative thought to enable you have a better and positive view of the world.

- Notice a shift in your attitude and don't forget that even if you have negative feelings and thoughts, they don't define you.

Getting to the Heart of the Stress

Stress does not usually come from a situation, rather, from your lower brain activity of catastrophizing the event and also jumping into several unrealistic worst-case scenarios. Engaging in this practice will help you reach out to the root of what's truly stressing you out.

- Start with just a question- "What is it that am I really scared of?" Write down your answer on s paper (for instance, I'm afraid I don't have sufficient time to complete my project).

- Follow up with the next question; "If what I fear were really to be true, what would I have to be afraid of?" (e.g., I'm afraid my boss will be angry with me and it may affect my job if I don't deliver the job on time." Well, continue writing all the answers that come to your heart until you discover the root of your stress.

- Now, return to each statement and rephrase them not as fears but as facts (e.g., my boss will be angry with me and this may be unfavorable for my job). Ask yourself if each one of the fears is true. You will discover that most of the fears are amplified and they are not really as bad as you initially thought. So, stay positive and believe the best rather than the worst.

Clearing the Stress in just 3 Minutes

Meditation has proven to be an effective way to declutter your mind and using this meditation tool will do just that for you because it perfectly fits into your schedule. In fact, with as little as 3 minutes, you can successfully practice this meditation and work your way up to 2 minutes. It will help rewire your brain and help you achieve a stress-free, quiet and fully present experience.

- Take a comfortable sitting position and place your feet on the ground with your hands positioned in your lap.
- With your eyes closed, follow your breathing for a short while.
- Observe the thoughts and feelings in your mind-avoid judging or changing your thoughts.
- As you approach the end of the process, let the thoughts and feelings that you have be put aside. This will give room to the emergence of a deeper sense of self while gaining freedom from the thoughts.

Combating Anxiety Attacks with This Meditation

In the event that anxious thoughts hit you, remember, there is a 90-second window available, which is enough for you to intervene before encountering a reaction to stress that may last for almost an hour before you recover it. You can avoid a full-blown anxiety attack by engaging in this short meditation.

- When you observe that stressful thoughts are building up into s greater reaction, simply imagine a "clear button" located at the center of your palm.

- With the index finger of the other hand, go ahead and press the button.

- Press the button continuously while visualizing it alerting your stress response system that it's time to calm down.

- Count to three and as you do so, take a deep breath with each count and visualize each number as a color.

- While exhaling for the last time, let go of the stressor and come back to the present. You can repeat this process two or three times if one attempt does not help, practice it until it works for you.

Basically, none of these meditation tips will work if you don't make effort to practice them. If you must break the cycle of stress and anxiety, then you must be prepared to take action. As you progress, you will develop new habits that will replace your old habits of worrying and n. You will be able to change your focus from stressful thoughts and anxious feelings to a positive and calm one.

Chapter 8 Adopting a Positive Mindset and Resilience

Unknowingly to us, we have been cultivating our resilience skills all our lives. From our efforts to walk to running as a toddler, we have been cultivating the ability to thrive during challenging times and adversity our whole lives. Our bodies are programmed to go through several changes when we're stressed to allow us to become capable of handling every situation that we encounter daily.

We become faster, stronger and more alert as we grow and this enables us to deal with challenges daily. It's common for us to experience an increased heart rate, blood pressure and in certain situations, our stress hormones (cortisol) will pump through our body. The prefrontal cortex which is the area that controls the brain can actually be shut down temporarily due to stress and we need this region of our brain to solve problems regulate emotion and control our impulses. Therefore, how well the prefrontal cortex is activated depends on our resilience.

Also, our ability to provide solution when we are under stressful conditions to the stress we are currently experiencing, recover and adapt to life's challenges is greatly diminished. Each of us has different ways of responding, reacting and recovering from stressful events in our lives: It could be by becoming angry, withdrawing from the situation, being resentful, emotional or simply being motivated to do much better. I must point out that even the most resilient people also experience their down days. So, you need to build your resilience if you must break the cycle of stress and anxiety.

How to Build Your Resilience

The following points will help you develop resilience and be better equipped to deal with stressful events when they come because they must surely come someday.

Boost Your Confidence

You must consciously develop positive beliefs in abilities. Believe that you can do anything that your mind has set out to do provided that you must remain positive and optimistic.

The first step to achieving anything you want is to believe that it's achievable.

Build Stronger Social Networks

You need to build a stronger social network of people that are positive minded. Although having people who sincerely want the best for you and are supportive, caring and positive will not cause all your problems to disappear, it will provide you with a better solution because a problem shared is indeed half-solved. Your social network will be able to support you, provide positive feedback and also assist you in thinking of positive solutions to your problems.

Learn new Skills

You need problem-solving skills and also general skills. Learning should be a constant process for you because things will definitely change and through various opportunities and experiences in life, you will be able to gain new skills and improve on existing ones. As you continue to adopt new skills and adapt to the skills, you will continue the process of improving and this will make you more resilient

to changes that happen at home, at school or at work.   Be
Ready for Change- Always be flexible and ready to adapt.
When you are willing to adapt, you will be properly equipped
with the right tools you require to deal with any issue that
you may face along the way.

Also Consider Yourself

Most times, we easily neglect and ignore our needs especially
when we're stressed, however, this is not good for you. It
will lead to a decrease in your resilience when you need it
most. Some common reactions to stress include not sleeping
properly, losing appetite, not eating or not exercising well.
Learn to focus on yourself and create time for the things you
love like your hobbies. You will improve your health and
gain strength which will, in turn, improve the resilience you
need in a time of crises.

Always be Thankful

One powerful way to appreciate someone is by saying thank
you. Have you observed that sometimes, you expect people
to say thank you and other times, you may not even realize

that you desperately desire to hear it. When we are thanked, we are motivated because we believe that what we have been spending our time and effort on is paying off. So, how often do you really say thank you to other people? Take a look at some facts about saying thank you:

- Apart from making other people feel you have good manners, saying thank you also helps to strengthen relationships and when you appreciate people, it enables them to believe that you have good intentions and this will motivate them to seek an ongoing relationship. This fact was proven by a study which was published in 2014.

- **It helps to improve Your Psychological health**- It has been confirmed by a researcher Robert Emmons that gratitude reduces depression and increases happiness. It was discovered in a study that Vietnam War Veterans having greater levels of gratitude experienced lower levels of PTSD.

- **It strengthens Your Physical Health-** It has been discovered that people who are thankful, are motivated to exercise more often, experience less pains and aches and do their yearly checkups.

- **It makes you less Aggressive and More Empathetic-** A University of Kentucky study concluded that those who scored high on the gratitude scale were more empathetic and sensitive toward others and also less likely to retaliate even in cases where they received negative feedback.

- **Increases Self-Esteem-** By being thankful, you will reduce social comparisons and you will feel less resentful and jealous toward other people that have more than you do.

- **In Enhances Your Sleeping Habits-** Did you know that by writing on your mobile device or in a journal what made you happy, your favorite part of a day etc. has shown to increase your positivity and also enhance your sleep.

Embrace Happiness

If truly you want to be happy, then you need to cultivate a positive mindset and learn to be content. In our world, it's quite easier for us to worry about issues or challenges that may never happen and on the negative. When your focus is on just one negative thing, everything else will become blurred and in some cases, you may not notice the positives that are around you. Basically, there are three things that we are encouraged to do that will program our brain to help us search for positives in every situation easily and they include:

Maintaining a gratitude diary, giving compliments and doing one act of kindness each day. I guess you might say that it's quite easy to do, well, just go ahead and try it. Finding true happiness will never be possible if you fail to follow to practice these simple but effective tips. Happiness provides several benefits, it strengthens your immune system and generally improves your health. In fact, it has been discovered that happiness can uplift the moods of people around you and increase productivity. Remember,

"Every day may not be good, but there is something good in everyday"

It's practically impossible to be happy all the time because humans can feel 48 different emotions. The following tips are some scientifically proven tips that can help pull you out from unhappiness and help you stay happy

1. **Hugging-** It has been recommended that we should hug at least eight times in a day. Also, a handshake or a pat on the back can increase your level of happiness. They are capable of making a strong impact on the human psyche which makes us feel joy and happiness.

2. **Searching for your old personal photos-** Researchers at the Open University have concluded that you will feel 11 percent better by looking at your old photos from time to time.

3. **Shorten the Length of Your Commute-** After studying the diaries of several thousands of subjects that recorded their activities and emotions at different times each day, Princeton psychologist Daniel Kahneman discovered that "Commuting to work was very low on the happiness chart and he

concluded that people are generally in a terrible mood when they commute. In another study, a group of researchers discovered that a twenty-minute commute will tremendously improve moods. After observing 4,000 subjects, the subjects were asked to rate their level of happiness on a scale of one to five. They determined that one of the highest measurements of happiness was actually a shortened commute and it was also observed that people rated their happiness highest when their maximum time of commuting was a maximum of twenty minutes.

Chapter 9 Switching Off is Possible

Working is sometimes like a drug: you can become completely addicted to it. When working has become an addiction, you are at greater risk of getting a job-related illness such as stress and unhappiness or RSI. People who are addicted to their work are called workaholics. Not such a nice word: it seems to imply that people themselves are to blame for their Stress or RSI. This blame is not justified because the work pressure is always of more significance than personal characteristics. Without blaming yourself it is useful, however, to ask yourself why you continue to work so hard, why you cannot stop working. Why, for example, can you not take sick leave in time? And why do you never take all the holidays you are entitled to?

When you answer full of despair that you just can't stop working, it is useful to check whether there is work addiction at play. This is particularly important because addiction is a mechanism that is operating in its own right, and that does not go away once you stop working. The addiction would simply shift and you might find yourself engaging in several activities like shopping, surfing the internet with computer or mobile device for several hours, getting drunk on a daily basis or visiting the gym unnecessarily. In short, you end up doing something with the same drive as when you were working.

This is not the way to get better at all because your whole day is now characterized by achieving another goal. People who are recovering from the stress and who go to the gym, often report how they keep an eye on what the person next to them is doing: Am I faster? Am I sweating more? They are fixated on rowing, cycling or walking even faster. Whether they enjoy these activities is of secondary importance; for them what matters is the targets and the achievements.

You just have to turn off this process. And this is only possible by changing your attitude.

Not Being Able to do Without Your Job

One of the attractive sides of addiction is that it provides a kick or a high, which dulls unpleasant feelings and reduces tension. This goes for all kinds of addictions. Whether you are using drugs or alcohol, or are gambling at the slot machines, the pattern is the same. It means that you are away from this world for a while, you are released from yourself, and you can get totally involved in something that feels passionate and compelling. Freud described this as an oceanic feeling: for a little while just being one with the world. You can also have this experience when you are in love. The feeling lifts you above the dreary, sad, everyday experiences of rain, rubbish on the streets and noisy neighbors. As such there is nothing wrong with this feeling. We would all like to have that feeling. It comes close to the feeling that people who are engaged in sport describe as flow: being totally involved in a match and being lifted out of yourself for a moment. It is no longer so much a matter of winning, but you are absorbed in the process, in what you are achieving at that moment. It only becomes an addiction when you can no longer do without that experience when you feel anxious, confused and full of despair without that experience. You have no other choice, you have to work because otherwise, you feel as if you no longer count, no longer exist, and you are afraid that out of despair you will end your life. When you say to yourself or to others that you cannot do without your work, then you have already crossed the addiction boundary. Then withdrawal symptoms will set in at the time you intend to stop working simply because you are completely exhausted. You may become restless and also depressed. And on some rare occasions, people lose all contact with reality and may even become psychotic.

Why are you Addicted?

Addiction is a way of dealing with problems. You take refuge in your work; your job is a way of survival. People say how they have thrown themselves into their work after one of their loved ones died or after a divorce. When this survival behavior is temporary, it is not really a problem. But when you notice that you have become fully addicted to this adrenaline kick, then there is a problem. Henry, who is an interior designer, had already been burnt out for nearly two years when he started to get treatment. He no longer worked but was addicted to surfing the internet and to buying things.

121

Before the therapy session, he was sitting in the waiting room, looking through the magazines in a strange manner. He devoured the pictures; his gaze was totally fixated on them, his face and posture tense, and he frantically turned the pages as quickly as he could. It seemed as if he wanted to take in everything, and was angry because there were so many illustrations in the magazines. He displayed this obsessed attitude in all aspects of his life. When he started to note down all activities of the day, he noticed this, and it became possible to talk about it. He then began to change: he still did the same activities, but for shorter periods of time and often with less intensity. Not going shopping three times a day but only once; no longer at the computer in the evenings, but one hour during the day. In this way, he had time left to do activities he really enjoyed.

The journey towards finding joy did not commence instantaneously, as it necessitated breaking free from ingrained habits. Eventually, however, a sense of relaxation began to settle within him. Gradually, his perspective shifted from obsessive to attentive. He took the time to introspect and rediscover the activities he once found pleasure in. Painting, capturing photographs, immersing himself in music, and delving into books were among the endeavors that resonated with him. By carving out space for these pursuits within his daily routine, a newfound calmness embraced him, and a gradual return to appreciating life's simple pleasures unfolded.

In Henry's quest to conquer burnout, he unearthed a significant realization regarding the underlying cause of his addiction. In contrast to his family members who willingly embraced the family business, Henry boldly chose a path that diverged from the conventional route to immediate prosperity. Regrettably, his father perceived Henry as a disruptor to the family's legacy, subjecting him to immense pressure to forsake his chosen path and conform to the family business. Furthermore, his brothers mocked the modest car Henry owned, flaunting their lavish BMWs instead.

This relentless external scrutiny compelled Henry to prove himself in the realm of interior design. His burning desire was to demonstrate to his father that his decision was the right one, seeking to win his father's approval and validation. Henry pushed himself to the brink, physically and emotionally, in an arduous attempt to convince both his father and brothers that he was not a failure, sparing no effort or sacrifice.

He deflected the unpleasant feeling that his father disowned him, by becoming the black sheep of the family. In fact, he had not yet released himself from the parental approval. In this way the treatment was also a stepping stone to standing on his own two feet, to give direction to his life with his own compass.

How do you Handle Your Addiction?

The following three steps are needed:

1. Become aware that addiction is nothing more (but also nothing less!) than an attitude with which you do all everyday activities.
2. Reduce the activities you do as an addict (in other words, as a madman). Do them less intensively. In

the time that you free up in this way, go and do things you previously enjoyed. Plan your day, keep to that structure every day and keep a record of what you do in the day. Do not forget to be lazy.

3. What feelings arise when you are not rushing around? Do you feel sad, angry or fearful? Give space to these feelings, investigate them, and see if they are justified. On your own, or with the help of somebody else, try to process these feelings, so that you can let go of your past. Only when you let go, can you yourself determine the direction of your life again?

Chapter 10 Effectively Managing Your Time

Okay, one of the best strategies for switching off without affecting your productivity is to manage your time effectively. You can make use of the "Time Management Matrix" developed by Steven Covey in every aspect of your life. You can adopt it when going grocery shopping, taking your kids to school or replying to an email. When you use a time management model, you will become more efficient and effective in your daily endeavors.

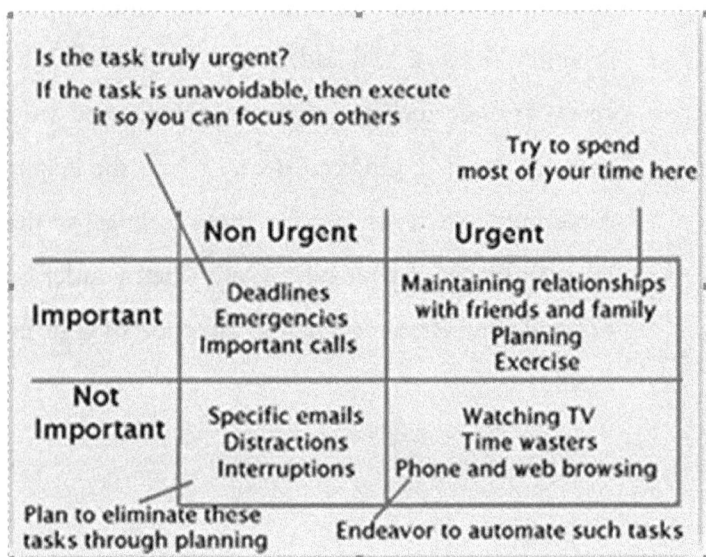

Is the task truly urgent?
If the task is unavoidable, then execute
it so you can focus on others

Try to spend
most of your time here

	Non Urgent	Urgent
Important	Deadlines Emergencies Important calls	Maintaining relationships with friends and family Planning Exercise
Not Important	Specific emails Distractions Interruptions	Watching TV Time wasters Phone and web browsing

Plan to eliminate these
tasks through planning

Endeavor to automate such tasks

You need to learn to focus on how important and urgent a task is and remember, if your task is none of the two, then you don't have to bother yourself much. Every one of us has been programmed in a way that we believe some things in our lives are far more important that they truly are. Ask yourself this simple yet profound question. Why do we hear the buzz of our phone and suddenly feel that we need to respond to it immediately yet we can postpone our trip to the gym even when going to the gym is no doubt more important than having to reply a message that's probably talking about a dinner venue.

Tips to help you Prioritize

In order to reduce the amount of time you have to waste in doing tasks that are not important, you can work with the following tips:

- **First you need to Turn off your Phone Notifications-** It may be difficult at first, however, you can start with few hours daily and extend it as you feel more comfortable. By turning off your phone notification, you will be able to reduce the amount of time you waste every time you get distracted.

- **Learn to Say no more Often-** You must get used to saying no sometimes, in fact, saying no is not selfish but selfless. I'll talk about saying no later in this chapter.

- **Have a to-do-list Daily-** You have to decide early at the beginning of the day which job is important and which job is urgent.

- **It's perfectly Okay to ignore some Tasks until Later-** This does not mean that you're rude, you have to ensure that you're not wasting time on the tasks that are not crucial in getting the tasks you have to get done, done.

- **Learn to Focus-** You should learn to focus one to three tasks each day so you can give full attention to each of the tasks.

In order to effectively handle several tasks, you need to learn to effectively manage your time. It helps you reduce long-term stress by providing you with a direction when there are so many tasks to accomplish. You will be able to stay in control of your tasks and increase your productivity. You will be able to create time for relaxation when you effectively manage your time. In order to manage your time effectively, you should learn to:

- Prioritize better
- Delegate tasks to other people
- Plan better
- You should have control over your environment

Saying No

We often view the word no as negative, however, it's just about our perception. Most people feel that saying no is being selfish, however, saying worse is usually a worse option in most cases. When you say yes and fail to deliver the best you can, you will end up giving a low-quality service, effort or time which will end up being more upsetting. Just remember, it's possible for you to do anything you want but it's absolutely impossible to do everything. When you say yes all the time, you will end up being tired, worn out and stressed and this usually causes you to be down or even expose you to illness.

Our body's immune system is our main defense system and whenever you are stressed, it will negatively affect how well your body will be able to fight off viruses, bacteria, and germs. Consequently, this will affect other commitments you have negatively and this could cause you to finally say no to things that are more important. Rather than allowing the situation to get to this point simply because you're scared of saying no to someone, you can save yourself the stress by saying no and not feeling bad about it.

Technology Use, Depression, Fatigue, and Stress

One of the greatest ways to break the cycle of stress, depression, and anxiety is to change your attitude toward technology. In fact, our sleep is greatly disturbed by technological devices since the artificial light emitted from computers, TVs, and mobile devices negatively impacts on melatonin production, which in turn, disrupts the circadian rhythm leading to a disturbance of the deep and restorative sleep that we seriously need. According to researchers at the University of Gothenburg, Sweden, it was discovered that the intensive use of computers, cell phones can be associated with an increase in sleep disorders, stress and depressive symptoms in young adults. The findings of the research include:

- Men that intensively make use of computers have a higher chance of developing sleeping problems

- There was an increase in sleep disorders in men due to the heavy use of phones while both men and women witness an increase in depressive symptoms.

- The regular and late night use of the computer was linked with sleep disorders, depressive symptoms in women and men and an increase in stress

- People that were constantly accessible through their cell phones stand an increased chance of reporting mental health problems

- The association gets much stronger with the combination of heavy mobile device use and heavy computer use

- Using the computer frequently without interruption further leads to an increase in the risk of sleeping problems, depressive symptoms, and stress in women.

Obviously, the health issues caused by the use of such devices has become serious. When the light from the screen of these devices affects the production of melanopsin simulation and melatonin, it disrupts the human circadian rhythms which in turn prevents or interrupts deep and restorative sleep leading to an increase in depressive and stress symptoms. So what's the way forward? You need to take steps to protect your health from the negative effects of technology. You must make efforts to turn off all mobile devices including your TV and computer and get a good sleep. While in the office or at home working on your computer, endeavor to take frequent breaks and don't forget to restrict the amount of time you normally spend online. Remember, if you don't post on Facebook, your followers will definitely wait for you until you're ready.

Chapter 11 Sleep as a Strategy for Dealing with Anxiety, Stress, and Depression

In order to completely break free from the cycle of anxiety, stress, and unhappiness, you need to also work on your sleep. You must endeavor to improve both the quality and quantity of your sleep. So, why exactly is sleep important? Although the answer may be obvious, however, there are several ways sleep can increase your stress and anxiety. Sleep debt is known to lead to anxiety even in people that don't frequently experience anxiety. Several health issues may arise when you don't get enough sleep and sleep debt tends to even affect people already experiencing anxiety most and this makes it much difficult for them to cope with several symptoms. Apart from causing stress, sleep debt can lead to other health issues that can increase the symptoms of anxiety.

What you may know is that when you don't sleep well, it may lead to anxiety. However, what you may not have considered is that sleep debt leads to the inability of your body to relieve the high level of stress that you might have encountered during the day while working. Sleep is the mechanism with which the body repairs itself and also relaxes the muscle tensions that accumulated during the day. Without sufficient sleep, your stress level will continue to mount and this may cause you to find it difficult dealing with stress the next day.

How sleep deprivation Causes Anxiety

Let's take a look at some ways sleep deprivation can lead to stress:

1. **Causes Body Stress-** The first and major effect of sleep debt is body stress. There is a mind and body connection which implies that stress to your body will negatively lead to stressful thoughts so when your body lacks the chance to heal, stress immediately starts building up fast.

2. **Causes Stress to Your Brain-** Several studies have also revealed that sleep deprivation affects the brain. Those who suffer sleep deprivation experience major brain "dysfunctions" which can further lead to anxiety, in fact, the brain will start hallucinating and

experience several symptoms (emotional and mental) that are similar to paranoid schizophrenia. The reason why this happens is still unclear, however, it is believed that while we sleep, the brain regenerates neurons which affect different areas of emotion, health and thought and when we fail to sleep, these neurons will not regenerate and may actually stop firing in some cases.

Scientists have discovered that some areas of the human brain such as the entire temporal lobe can actually turn off in the event that the brain does not get sufficient sleep. This kind of reaction can cause two problems when it comes to sleep and anxiety: It is most likely that the areas of the brain that are responsible for controlling "coping" will be turned off. Second, the possibility of your brain suffering from more generic tension and stress will increase because your brain will work harder just to make up for other areas that have possibly stopped working.

Brain stress can also lead to anxiety so as much as you can, avoid.

3. **Leads to Physical Symptoms-** Your body can experience serious unusual physical symptoms when it doesn't get enough sleep, in fact, you may discover that your nerves may fire in strange ways while your arms and legs may tingle at different times. Also, you may experience backaches or headaches and some sensations and weird pains in various parts of your body. This situation can be quite stressful for those with anxiety especially panic attacks. Most physical symptoms mimic serious diseases and this gets even worse for those with anxiety when their sleep debt increases. For people having some sleep, it can be tricky because they may feel rested but are not getting the right quantity and quality of sleep. While they may enjoy the cognitive functioning of people that slept well, their body may still react as if they didn't sleep at all and this leads to fear for those with panic attacks about other health issues.

Dealing with the Sleep Debt-Related Anxiety

Well, if you find yourself in this position, I have compiled several tips that will help you stop sleep debt that's linked to anxiety. The first thing you should have in mind is that the solution to sleep debt is getting more sleep. You can easily solve the problem by getting enough sleep whenever possible. Although it won't stop anxiety immediately, it will set the pace for your recovery. Sleep debt issues seem to linger and to effectively stop is, you may have to get a good quantity and quality of sleep for some weeks at a time. You must consciously go to bed earlier else, you will still experience the anxiety. Also, there are cases where you're finding it difficult to sleep especially because of the sleep deprivation anxiety making it difficult to rest, then the following techniques will help you regain your ability to sleep.

Change Your Locations

If you've been struggling with sleep for an extended period of time, you might consider changing your bed because it might no longer represent the comfortable place you need. In some cases, your bed may be linked with stress, so you have to endeavor to break such association. You can find another place to sleep instead of your bed, like a comfy chair or couch. You can sleep there for some time until you feel comfortable enough to go back to your bed.

Practice Journal Writing

Most times, the reason why anxiety keeps you awake is because of some troubling thoughts that have occupied your head that you find difficult to ignore. Although the thought might not be stressful, it may engage your mind and provide you with something to focus on. One way to let go of some thoughts that are stopping you from sleeping is to write it down in a journal near you. When you do so, your brain will immediately be signaled to forget about the thought since it has been recorded in a permanent location (journal). This strategy calms the active minds of some people and you should consider trying it.

Get New Routines

Sometimes, all you need is just some boring pre-sleep routines that may be annoying in some ways. First, you should turn off all gadgets and bright lights in your room, then proceed to engage yourself in something boring and slow at home. Try to repeat the same things for days until they become a habit or routine. After some weeks, your mind will be used to the idea that the routines indicate sleeping time and this immediately helps you to relax

Ensure that your bedroom is quiet, dark and cool. In case of an excess noise, you can drown out the noise with a fan. Your bedroom should be a bedroom for sleeping and sex, you shouldn't turn it into a cinema where you watch the TV. Form the habit of getting into bed only when you're tired and feeling sleepy. It is estimated that we need between seven to nine hours of sleep daily, so if you're not getting up to that amount of sleep, you have to create more time for sleep. This will require making serious life changes which will help secure your health and increase your productivity. Other things you should avoid before sleeping are stimulants like nicotine, coffee, and chocolate. Engaging in regular exercise can also help in setting you in the mood for sleep but ensure your exercise time does not come close to sleeping time.

Final Thoughts

Recent trends in our society have proven that the impact of stress and anxiety has caused many people to live unhappy lives and in some cases, people have become depressed. Anxiety and depression affect both men and women, the young and old, professionals, students, housewives and even businessmen. The impact of stress and anxiety has led to marital discord, interpersonal conflicts poor performance at work and school, and generally a sense of being worthless and isolated. Having read through this book, I'm sure you have gained so much information on how to break the cycle of stress and anxiety in your life.

I know that you are serious about breaking free from anxiety and stress and that's why you were able to read up to this point. I'll suggest that you read the book again to grasp the information better and practice the things you've learned from the book. Create more time for yourself and your family and by doing that, you will reduce the stress you experience in life. Always remember that hope, determination, faith, and patience are the great tools needed to do break free from anxiety because you will need faith and determination to be able to read this book and put to work what you have read. You will require hope and patience to see it produce the much-expected results and remember, giving up is not an option.

Breaking the cycle of anxiety and stress will not happen in a day or a week, it requires time and you need to be patient while changing your lifestyle to reduce stress and anxiety.

About the Author

Author: Harib Shaqsy.

He is the author of the best seller book "Hard Work Can Keep You Poor." In his book, Harib feels that most people are over working and over stressed unnecessarily, because, they believe that working hard is the only way to survive, be paid more and become richer, he explains why this is not true in his book.

You can also check some of Harib's work available in bookshops and online.

Visit website: http://haribshaqsy.com